JOHN PAUL II
WORDS OF INSPIRATION

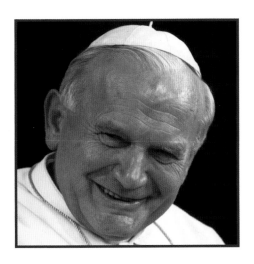

First published 2003 by Contender Books

Contender Books is a division of
The Contender Entertainment Group
48 Margaret Street
London W1W 8SE
www.contendergroup.com/books

This edition © Contender Ltd 2003

1 3 5 7 9 10 8 6 4 2

Edited by Lesley Young

All rights reserved.

Picture credits: Front cover © Rex features/halstead/timepix; P14 & 16 © Sonia Halliday
Photographs, photos by David Silverman; p9, 22 & 48 © Iberpress/Andes Press Agency;
p29 © Alpha/Lapresse; p54 © PA Photos; p63 © PA Photos/EPA; back cover photo
© PA Photos/DPA. All other images supplied by Corbis Ltd.

ISBN 1-84357-071-8

Designed by seagulls

Printed in Italy

Life is the time that is granted to us to express concretely the potential riches which each of us bears and to make our contribution to the common progress of mankind. Life is the time that is given to us to embody in ourselves and in history the values of love, goodness, joy, justice, and peace, to which the human heart aspires.

Ultimately, only God can save man, but He expects man to co-operate.

Man feels the inner need to transcend himself. Only in transcending himself does man become fully human.

It is very important to cross the threshold of hope, not to stop before it, but to let oneself be led.

There is every reason for the truth of the Cross to be called the Good News.

Man affirms himself most completely by giving of himself. This is the fulfillment of the commandment of love. This is also the full truth about man.

Only the one who is able to be demanding with himself in the name of love can also demand love from others. Love is demanding. Nowadays people need to rediscover this demanding love, for it is the truly firm foundation of the family, a foundation able to 'endure all things.'

Singing is a particularly apt way to express a joyful heart, accentuating the solemnity of the celebration and fostering the sense of a common faith and a shared love.

Christ has the answer
to your questions and the
key to history; he has
the power to uplift hearts.

The splendour of Christ's glory is reflected in the face of every human being, and is even more so when that face is emaciated by hunger, saddened by exile, or oppressed by poverty and misery.

Jesus Christ has taken the lead on the way of the cross. He has suffered first. He does not drive us towards suffering but shares it with us, wanting us to have life and to have it in abundance.

We need to turn to Christ, the Word of God who became flesh for humanity's salvation.

Prayer can truly change your life. For it turns your attention away from yourself and directs your mind and your heart toward the Lord. If we look only at ourselves, with our own limitations and sins, we quickly give way to sadness and discouragement. But if we keep our eyes fixed on the Lord, then our hearts are filled with hope, our minds are washed in the light of truth, and we come to know the fullness of the Gospel with all its promise and life.

It is right to fight sickness because health is a gift of God. At the same time, it is also important to be able to interpret God's plan when suffering knocks at our door.

Not only does God have a divine heart, rich in mercy and in forgiveness, but also a human heart, capable of all the stirrings of affection.

*True happiness lies
in giving ourselves in
love to our brothers
and sisters.*

Christ looks with love upon every human being.

The world is not able to free man from suffering; specifically it is not able to free him from death.

Between the finger of God and the finger of man stretching out to each other and almost touching, there seems to leap an invisible spark: God communicates to man a tremor of his own life, creating him in his own image and likeness. That divine breath is the origin of the unique dignity of every human being, of humanity's boundless yearning for the infinite.

Immortality is not a part of this world. It can come to man exclusively from God.

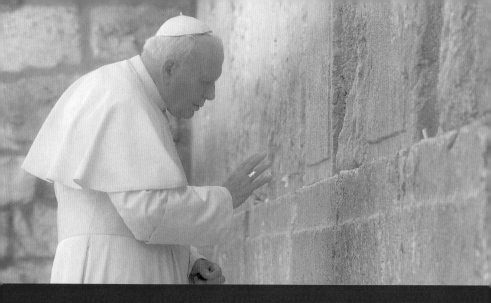

Everyone must respect the inviolable limits that reference to morality can offer us. When men and women lose their sense of these limits and set themselves up as legislators for the world, they forget that they are on this earth like the grass and the flowers of the field that fade away.

When our road seems hard and laborious, when fear and anxiety seem to prevail, it is especially then that the Word of God should be our light and our strong support.

We must see another's poverty as our own and be convinced that the poor can wait no longer.

There is no evil to be faced that Christ does not face with us. There is no enemy that Christ has not already conquered. There is no cross to bear that Christ has not already borne for us, and does not now bear with us.

For Christians, Sunday is the fundamental feast day, established not only to mark the succession of time but to reveal time's deeper meaning. Saint Basil explains that Sunday symbolizes that truly singular day which will follow the present time, the day without end which will know neither evening or morning, the imperishable age which will never grow old; Sunday is the ceaseless foretelling of life without end which renews the hope of Christians and encourages them on their way.

The power of Christ's Cross and Resurrection is greater than any evil which man could or should fear.

The person created in the image and likeness of God, exists 'for his own sake' and reaches fulfilment precisely by sharing in God's life.

Any threat to human rights, whether in the field of material realities or in that of spiritual realities, is equally dangerous for peace, since in every instance it concerns man in his entirety.

The image of Christ on the Cross, the price of the redemption of humanity, is a pressing appeal to spend our lives in putting ourselves at the service of the needy, in harmony with charity, which is generous and which does not sympathize with injustice, but with truth.

Every man has inherent in him the mystery of a new life which Christ has brought and which he has grafted on to humanity.

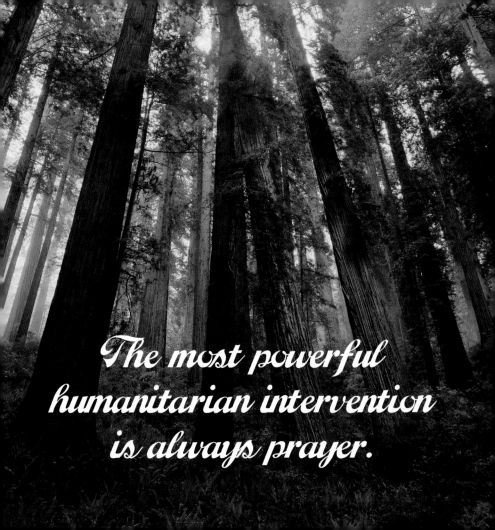

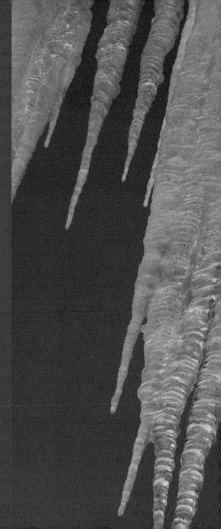

As in the days of swords and spears, so too today in the era of missiles, more than arms, it is the human heart which kills.

What really matters in life is that we are loved by Christ, and that we love him in return. In comparison to the love of Jesus, everything else is secondary. And without the love of Jesus, everything else is useless.

Confession is an act of honesty and courage; an act of entrusting ourselves, beyond sin, to the mercy of a loving and forgiving God. It is an act of the prodigal son who returns to his Father and is welcomed by him with the kiss of peace.

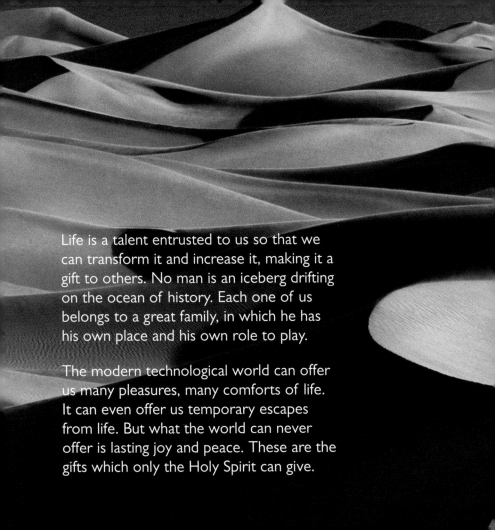

Life is a talent entrusted to us so that we can transform it and increase it, making it a gift to others. No man is an iceberg drifting on the ocean of history. Each one of us belongs to a great family, in which he has his own place and his own role to play.

The modern technological world can offer us many pleasures, many comforts of life. It can even offer us temporary escapes from life. But what the world can never offer is lasting joy and peace. These are the gifts which only the Holy Spirit can give.

In Christ you will discover the true greatness of your own humanity.

All creation is invited to sing to the Lord a new song, to rejoice and to exult together with all the nations of the earth.

Much more influential than the corruption present in the world is the divine power of the Sacrament of Confirmation.

In God is the fullness of glory and his earthly birth on Christmas night testifies once and for all that in him every man is included in the mystery of God's love, which is the source of definitive peace.

Let us praise the Lord! Let us praise him unceasingly. But our lives must express our praise, more than our words.

Even during the dark night we feel protected by God's wings.

Man lives at the same time both in the world of material values and in that of spiritual values. For the individual living and hoping man, his needs, freedoms and relationships with others never concern one sphere of values alone, but belong to both.

If we cannot accept the prospect of giving ourselves as a gift, then the danger of a selfish freedom will always be present.

Just as Mary visited Elizabeth, so you too are called to 'visit' the needs of the poor, the hungry, the homeless, those who are alone or ill.

We need the enthusiasm of the young. We need their joie de vivre.

The young know how to express this joy in their own special way.

Never forget that blindly following the impulse of our emotions often means becoming a slave to our passions.

A life reduced to the sole dimension of possessions, of consumer goods, of temporal concerns, will never let you discover and enjoy the full richness of your humanity.

Concern for the child, even before birth, from the first moment of conception and then throughout the years of infancy and youth, is the primary and fundamental test of the relationship of one human being to another.

Woman has an understanding, sensitive and compassionate heart that allows her to give a delicate, concrete style to charity.

Without Christ it is not possible to resolve issues which are daily becoming more complicated for the international institutions and organizations, as well as for the various governments involved in the conflict.

When a person is entirely open to the breath of God's love, he becomes caught up in a spiritual 'adventure' far beyond anything imaginable.

Christ taught us to forgive. He taught Peter to forgive 'seventy times seven times' (Mt. 18:22).

Without the reference to God – the whole world of created values remains as if it were suspended in an absolute vacuum.

Selfishness makes people dead and dumb; love opens eyes and hearts.

The vocation to love, understood as true openness to our fellow human beings and solidarity with them, is the most basic of all vocations. It is the origin of all vocations in life.

God loves you all, without distinction, without limit. He loves those of you who are elderly, who feel the burden of the years. He loves those of you who are sick, those of you suffering from AIDS and AIDS-related complex. He loves the relatives and friends of the sick and those who care for them. He loves us all with an unconditional and everlasting love.

Prayer represents an enormous spiritual power, especially when accompanied by sacrifice and suffering... Even if it is not apparent to a superficial glance and many people do not acknowledge it, prayer joined to sacrifice constitutes the most powerful force in human history.

Youth should be 'growth'.
For this purpose, contact with
the visible world, with nature,
is of immense importance.

Down through the centuries and generations it has been seen that in suffering there is concealed a particular power that draws a person interiorly close to Christ, a special grace.

The more a person is threatened by sin, the heavier the structures of sin which today's world brings with it, the greater is the eloquence which human suffering possesses in itself. And the more the Church feels the need to have recourse to the value of human sufferings for the salvation of the world.

This is the truth that the Church never tires of proclaiming: God loves us with an infinite love.

The person who is a 'neighbour' cannot indifferently pass by the suffering of another: this in the name of fundamental human solidarity, still more in the name of love of neighbour.

The faithful realize that they are little ones, who are poor and in great need of God's help, and they come together to receive the Messiah who is about to come. He will come in the silence, the humility, the poverty of the crib, and will bring his joy to all who welcome him with open hearts.

Be faithful to the truth and to its transmission, for truth endures; truth will not go away. Truth will not pass or change.

Keep Jesus
Christ in your
hearts, and you
will recognize
his face in every
human being.
You will want
to help him out
in all his needs:
the needs of
your brothers
and sisters.

Life is the time that is granted to us to express concretely the potential riches which each of us bears and to make our contribution to the common progress of mankind. Life is the time that is given to us to embody in ourselves and in history the values of love, goodness, joy, justice, and peace, to which the human heart aspires.

The Church counters the culture of death with the culture of love.

Love is true when it creates the good of persons and of communities; it creates that good and gives it to others.

Lord, grant us patience, serenity and courage; grant us to live in joyful charity, for love of You, with those who are suffering more than ourselves and with those who, though not suffering, have not a clear view of the meaning of life.

The human person's very existence in dignity and his or her rightful participation in the life of the community are safeguarded by the deep respect that every person entertains for the dignity and the rights of every fellow human being.

The Pope
bows with
devotion
before old
age, and he
invites all
people to
do the same
with him.

The love which the Apostle Paul celebrates in the First Letter to the Corinthians—the love which is 'patient' and 'kind', and 'endures all things' (1 Cor 13:4, 7)—is certainly a demanding love. But this is precisely the source of its beauty: by the very fact that it is demanding, it builds up the true good of man and allows it to radiate to others.

Mother of fair love, pray for us! Teach us to love God and our brothers, as you loved them: make our love for others to be always patient, kindly, respectful.

Do not be afraid of risks! God's strength is always far more powerful than your difficulties!

Jesus' dwelling is wherever a human person is suffering because rights are denied, hopes betrayed, anxieties ignored.

One could say that by being in contact with nature we absorb into our own human existence the very mystery of creation which reveals itself to us through the untold wealth and variety of visible beings, and which at the same time is always beckoning us towards what is hidden and invisible.

When we feel loved,
we ourselves are more
disposed to love.

*In the life of
every nation,
social progress
and human
development
are ensured by
the respect
given to the
rights of the
human person.*

Man exists not 'for death', but 'for immortality'.

May the Lord Jesus be always with you!
With his truth that makes you free (Jn 8:32);
with his word that unlocks the mystery of
man and reveals to man his own humanity;
with his death and Resurrection that makes
you new and strong.

Old age is the crown of the steps of life.
It gathers in the harvest, the harvest from
what you have learned and experienced,
the harvest from what you have done and
achieved, the harvest from what you have
suffered and undergone. As in the finale of a
great symphony, all the great themes of life
combine to a mighty harmony.

The physical and at the same time spiritual
nature of conjugal communion, always
enlightened by personal love, must lead to
respect for sexuality, its fully human dimension,
and never to use it as an 'object', in order not
to dissolve the personal union of soul and body.

Love reaches its peak in the gift the person makes of himself, without reserve, to God and to his brothers and sisters.

The painful experience of the history of my own country, Poland, has shown me how important natural sovereignity is when it is served by a state worthy of the name and free in its decisions; how important it is for the protection not only of a people's legitimate material interests but also of its culture and its soul.

Creating man and woman in his own image and likeness, God wills for them the fullness of good, or supernatural happiness, which flows from sharing in his own life.

We cannot live without love.
If we do not encounter love,
if we do not experience it
and make it our own, and
if we do not participate
intimately in it, our life
is meaningless.